SEEKING THE KINGDOM

CHARLES E. GRANT

Dedication

I give all glory to our Lord & Savior, Jesus Christ, who has truly redeemed my life and revealed to me purpose and destiny by way of the **Kingdom Message**. I'm genuinely convinced that the principles of the **Kingdom of God** are the answer to all mankind's problems.

Most people who were trying to share this message with me made me feel condemned or lost, especially those bound by religion.

Some messages I had heard were inspiring, encouraging, empowering, and uplifting, yet I didn't understand what they were trying to get me to see.

The **Kingdom Message** reveals the true purpose & destiny for all humanity. That is why it's called the **"Good News."** there is no more condemnation for those in Christ Jesus's dominion.

The **Kingdom Message** reveals the original purpose for all mankind; it empowers us to be what God created us to be.

"Seeking the Kingdom" is a journey. However, once found, it's the best thing anyone can encounter.

So, let us continue to **"Seek the Kingdom"** together, as the creator of all things reveals to us our purpose & destiny.

"The More We Seek the More Will Be Revealed"

There are so many **Ambassadors/Representatives** of the **Kingdom of God** who represent our heavenly Father. I can't list all who have been a tremendous blessing and contributor to my search for the **"Kingdom of God."**

I am grateful to all the people of God who have positively influenced me during this journey.

I dedicate this book to my Lovely Wife, Brenda ("The Real Deal") Grant, and all 6 of my children, LaMitchal, Charles Jr, Edward, Junior, Michael, and Ashley. I give God the glory for my Children, grandchildren, and entire Family.

My sincere prayer is that all come to understand the Kingdom of God as they continue to build relations with our Lord and Savior Jesus Christ (Holy Spirit) as our helper, teacher, guide, and mentor in the Kingdom of God.

"May God Continue to Bless You All Real Good."

Matthew 6:33 **(AMP)**

But first and most importantly, seeking **(aim at, strive after)** His Kingdom and his righteousness **(His way of doing and being right-the attitude and character of God),** and all these things will be given to you also.

His kingdom and his righteousness,"

His kingdom and righteousness are drawn into a profound understanding of God's divine nature and the essence of His kingdom. It signifies not only the sovereignty and dominion that God holds over all creation but also encompasses the very core of His character. His righteousness, which encircles His way of doing and being right, reflects the perfect alignment of His thoughts, actions, and intentions with His divine will. It is through this righteousness that God establishes His kingdom on earth, inviting believers to embrace His attitudes, values, and principles.

After more than 25 years of seeking, studying, and exploring the Word of God, I realize our purpose and destiny are revealed in seeking the Kingdom of God and His righteousness. I want to share what was revealed to me and pray that those who read **"Seeking the Kingdom"** come to realize their purpose and destiny in life and continue to explore the Kingdom of God.

Also, I want to encourage all believers of the **"Gospel"** of our Lord & Savior Jesus Christ, the **"Kingdom of God."** it's real…

Written by: **Charles E. Grant**

Inspiration by the Holy Spirit

About the Author

I'm a mere vessel in the Kingdom whom God has called out to preach the **"Kingdom Message"** of our Lord & Savior Jesus Christ, *"truly grateful for it."*

Charles E. Grant was Born in Chicago, IL, and raised on the south side of Chicago. I moved to Milwaukee, WI, at the age of 30. I lived there for about 15 years, underwent a transformation, then moved back to Chicago, IL.

I could never have imagined this message was real after over 25 years of living a life outside of the will of God and not having a clue about my purpose.

I'm truly grateful for what our Lord & Savior, Jesus Christ, has done for me and all humanity. For many years, I've studied the scriptures and asked questions regarding life in general, but it wasn't revealed to me until I began to understand the **"Kingdom Message."**

Throughout my life, I have heard many preachers and teachers preaching inspirational messages, but I didn't know what they were trying to get me to see regarding the **"Kingdom of God."**

For over 25 years, I have been assisting pastors in sharing the **"Good News,"** which is the gospel according to Jesus Christ. Jesus' purpose was to preach the **"Kingdom of God."**

In **Matthew 10:7,** Jesus said, "And **as you go**, preach, saying, the **kingdom of heaven** is at hand." **Luke 4:43** says, "But he said. "I must preach **(the good news of) the**

Kingdom of God to the other cities also because **I was sent for this purpose."**

In Matthew 10:7, Jesus delivers a powerful message, urging his disciples to go forth and spread the word that the kingdom of God is at hand. This verse resonates with me as it reminds me of my calling and responsibility to share the message of God's kingdom. Just as Jesus called upon his disciples to preach, I am instructed to follow in their footsteps and proclaim the kingdom's presence in my life.

This verse encourages me to actively engage with others, sharing the hope and love that comes from embracing the teachings of Christ. It reminds me that I have a role to play in bringing others closer to the kingdom of God and that through my words and actions, I can make a positive impact on those around me.

Introduction

I was called to preach over 20 years ago. During that time, I was encouraged by my pastor's wife (**1st lady of the Church**) to attend seminary. She paid for my 1st class and told me, "When the Lord calls and fills you with the Holy Spirit, make sure you continue to feed your spirit with the Word of God, and you will always have the Word of God to share with people."

I enrolled in seminary and studied several topics: the Old & New Testament Survey, the 4 Gospels, the Life of Jesus, the Life of Paul, theology, leadership, evangelism, etc., to name a few. I graduated with honors at the top of my class. I continued my studies, attending various conferences, seminars, and anything that would educate me in my quest for the truth as I found it in the word of God.

I was instructed to seek the Word of God, and every class, seminar, and conference I attended was revealing. But when I started going through some real-life challenges, I began to question God and found myself genuinely seeking.

Why? Why am I here? What is my purpose? Who am I? Why is this? Why is that? Where did I come from? I had so many questions about life in general. Then something happened to me; it was like the words of the scriptures jumped off the pages into my heart. I realized what the scriptures were referring to and what the Lord Jesus said and told me to seek after.

Matthew 6:33 teaches us to **first** and, most importantly, **seek (aim at, strive after) His Kingdom** and His

Righteousness **(His way of doing and being right - the attitude and character of God),** and all these things will be given to you also.

Seeking the kingdom first encompasses the idea of prioritizing it above all else. It signifies recognizing its significance as a principle that should guide our actions and decisions. By placing the kingdom as our highest value, we acknowledge its importance in shaping our lives. Seeking the kingdom as our highest value means actively pursuing, studying, exploring, and understanding its teachings and principles. It requires a commitment to making it our primary focus, allowing it to inform and direct our choices in all aspects of life. It is through this dedicated pursuit that we can truly embody the essence of seeking the kingdom first.

During my tenure as a student in seminary, all the classes, seminars, and conferences I attended were good. Still, none of these educational venues taught me about the **Kingdom of God**. So, I started seeking the **Kingdom of God** as Jesus commanded. Once I began seeking the Kingdom of God, the Lord reveal**ed the answers to all my questions.**

My understanding of the scriptures began to grow steadily. I began to understand Who I am, my purpose for existence, and why I was created. God started showing me "Me" through the concepts of a Kingdom.

To effectively communicate the "Good News" to others, it is imperative to have a deep understanding of the principles that govern the Kingdom **of God. At its core, the kingdom of God** emphasizes love, compassion, and justice. Love is the foundational principle, as it encourages individuals to treat one another with kindness and respect, mirroring the unconditional love that God has for all. Compassion follows closely, urging believers to show empathy and understanding towards others, especially those who are marginalized or in need of a savior. The Word of God **guides us, providing us with a roadmap to comprehend these principles**

. By immersing ourselves in the gospel's teachings, we gain insights into the values, beliefs, and ideals that shape the kingdom. This knowledge enables us to communicate with clarity and conviction, allowing others to grasp the transformative power of the Good News. Without a solid foundation in the Word of God and its principles, our message may lack depth and fail to resonate with those seeking spiritual direction.

People are looking for or seeking solutions to the issues in life. The answer to all humanity's problems lies in understanding the **Kingdom of God**. Having correct concepts of the kingdom's message is critical to understanding so there will not be any misconceptions about the message that I have been called to preach or teach.

Over 4,000 years ago, God promised us the coming of the Messiah **(Jesus)** or the crushing of the enemy's head by his seed.

Genesis 3:15 And I will put enmity between thee and the woman, and between thy seed and her seed; it shall bruise thy head, and thou shalt bruise his heel.

We understand this to refer to the coming of the Messiah **(Jesus)**. I often wondered why it took the Lord so long to reveal this promise.

Well, God is a God of timing. Throughout history, we see instances where God's timing played a crucial role in unveiling his divine plan. From the birth of Jesus Christ to the spread of Christianity, God's timing has been impeccable. It is through these carefully orchestrated moments that the kingdom of God has been revealed to humanity. This divine timing not only demonstrated God's sovereignty but also helped me to understand the importance of patience and trust in my pursuit of the kingdom. Just as God's timing has been evident in the **past, I found peace in knowing that he will continue to reveal his kingdom in his own perfect time.**

For example, **Isaiah 9:6** *For to us a Child shall be born, to us a Son shall be given; And the government shall be upon His shoulder, And His name shall be called Wonderful Counselor, Mighty God, Everlasting Father, Prince of Peace. 7: There shall be no end to the increase of his government and of peace (He shall rule) on the throne of David and over his kingdom, to establish it and to uphold it with justice and righteousness from that time forward and forevermore. The zeal of the Lord of hosts will accomplish this.*

As I began to understand the concepts of a Kingdom, it was revealed to me there had to be a prototype of a Kingdom society in the earth's realm, and the timing had to be perfect for God to reveal the **Kingdom of God**.

The concept of a Kingdom or prototype is crucial in understanding the fulfillment of God's promise through Jesus. For God to reveal his kingdom, there needed to be a foundational understanding of what a Kingdom entails. The idea of a Kingdom provides a framework, a blueprint if you will, for God to manifest his divine plan and establish his reign on earth. By allowing the Roman Empire to exist as a concept of a Kingdom, God strategically set the stage for the revelation of His own Kingdom through Jesus Christ.

Throughout history, empires have often been seen as symbols of power and authority, and the Roman Empire was no exception. By utilizing this familiar framework, God captured the attention and understanding of the people of that time. Furthermore, the Roman Empire's prominence allowed for the spreading of ideas and communication across vast territories, facilitating the rapid dissemination of Jesus' teachings and the message of God's Kingdom. In this way, God fulfilled His promise by using the existing concept of a Kingdom to bring about a deeper understanding and realization of His divine plan.

It is also important to note that the arrival of Jesus Christ was intricately tied to the Roman Empire, as it occurred when the empire held considerable power and influence over the region. The Roman Empire, known for its vast territorial expansion and political dominance, had established control over Judea, the birthplace of Jesus.

This connection is significant because it shaped the historical and cultural backdrop against which Jesus' teachings and actions unfolded. Additionally, the Roman occupation of Judea brought about a complex socio-political climate characterized by tensions between the ruling Roman authorities and the Jewish population.

Jesus' message of love, compassion, and spiritual salvation resonated with many individuals within this context, as it provided hope and peace amidst the challenges faced under Roman rule. Furthermore, the crucifixion of Jesus by the Romans marked a pivotal moment in his life and teachings, ultimately leading to his resurrection and the spread of Christianity throughout the Roman Empire and beyond. Thus, Jesus' coming was undeniably intertwined with the Roman Empire, influencing his mission and subsequent impact on history.

Notice the terminologies used in scripture; they always refer to a Kingdom, King, Lord, Etc. The Lord Jesus refers to himself as King, King of Kings, and Lord of Lords. Jesus' use of this terminology created a problem within the Roman Empire. His teachings and actions challenged the authority and power of both the political and religious leaders of Rome. Jesus preached about a new kingdom, the Kingdom of God, which posed a direct threat to the Roman Empire's claim of being the ultimate authority.

Moreover, his popularity among the masses and his ability to gather large crowds raised concerns among Roman officials, who feared that Jesus could potentially incite rebellion or civil unrest. Furthermore, Jesus' message of love, compassion, and equality contradicted the hierarchical structure and oppressive practices of Roman society. As a result, the Roman government viewed Jesus as a subversive figure who needed to be silenced in order to maintain control over its subjects.

That is why Jesus did not come to establish a physical kingdom or a religious group but rather to proclaim the Kingdom of God. This perspective challenges conventional notions of kingship and religious institutions, emphasizing a more profound spiritual realm. Jesus' teachings and actions consistently emphasized the presence and accessibility of God's Kingdom within individuals and society rather than focusing on establishing a physical dominion.

By declaring the **Kingdom of God**, Jesus invited people to seek a higher purpose and a transformative relationship with God, transcending the limitations of earthly power and religious structures. Thus, understanding Jesus' mission as centered on proclaiming the **Kingdom of God** opens doors to exploring the significance of personal spiritual growth and communal harmony in our pursuit of divine truth.

It is important to note that exploring the significance of personal spiritual growth and communal harmony in our pursuit of divine truth is a profound endeavor that encompasses individual introspection and collective unity. Personal spiritual growth entails the development of one's inner self, the deepening of faith, and the cultivation of a meaningful connection with the divine. It involves self-reflection, prayer, meditation, and engaging in spiritual practices that nourish the soul.

However, personal growth alone is not enough to fully grasp divine truth. Communal (Church) harmony plays a vital role in this pursuit as it fosters a sense of belonging, support, and shared wisdom. Through communal (Church) gatherings, spiritual teachings, and ministries, individuals can learn from one another's experiences, perspectives, and insights.

By embracing communal harmony, we create an environment that encourages open dialogue, empathy, and understanding among diverse individuals on their spiritual journeys. In essence, exploring personal spiritual growth alongside communal harmony allows us to navigate the vast realm of divine truth with humility, compassion, and a collective pursuit of enlightenment.

Jesus's message revolved around a Kingdom, specifically the Kingdom of God. In Matthew 10:7, he explicitly instructed his disciples to preach about this very kingdom. By proclaiming that "the kingdom of heaven is at hand," Jesus emphasized the imminence and accessibility of this divine realm. This statement suggests that the Kingdom of God was not a distant or abstract idea but rather a present reality that could be experienced and embraced by all who were willing to listen and follow his teachings. Thus, Jesus's message centered on the invitation to seek and enter into this kingdom, which embodied God's sovereignty, righteousness, and **eternal grace.**

Understanding the Kingdom's Message is not only a transformative experience, but it also holds the power to redeem us back to our original purpose for existence. As human beings, we were created in the image of God, meant to reflect His character and attributes in the world. However, as we navigate life's challenges and distractions, we often lose sight of this fundamental truth.

The Kingdom's message serves as a reminder, a compass that guides us back to our intended purpose. It illuminates the path of righteousness, compassion, and love that God desires us to walk upon. By understanding this message, we are empowered to live a life aligned with God's will and reflect His divine nature.

It is through this understanding that we find redemption, not only for ourselves but also for the world around us. In embracing the **Kingdom's Message, we become agents of change, bringing light into darkness and restoring hope where it has been lost. Matthew 4:23** And he went throughout all Galilee, teaching in their synagogues and preaching the good news **(gospel)** of the **kingdom**, and healing every kind of disease and every kind of sickness among the people **(demonstrating and revealing that he was indeed the promised Messiah).**

John the Baptist reveals the **Kingdom of Heaven** in his message and baptizes Jesus.

Matthew 3:1 In those days, John the Baptist appeared, preaching in the wilderness of Judah **(along the western side of the Dead Sea)** and saying,

2: Repent **(change your inner-self's old way of thinking, regret past sins, live your life in a way that proves repentance; seek God's purpose for your life),** for the **kingdom of heaven** is at hand".

Baptism represents submission in water to denote that we submit to the teaching or philosophy of another person **(Master Teacher).** John declares, "I baptize you with water for repentance. But after me comes one who is more powerful than I, whose sandals I am not worthy to carry. He will baptize you with the Holy Spirit and fire." Here, John emphasizes the distinction between his baptism of water and the future baptism that Jesus will administer. This scripture underscores John's role as a precursor to Jesus, preparing the way for His coming and laying the foundation for the significance of baptism within the Christian faith.

Jesus had a deep understanding of John's teachings and the importance of the kingdom of God. Recognizing the authority inherent in John's message, Jesus humbly submitted himself to this teaching, acknowledging its significance in his ministry. By aligning himself with the teaching of the **kingdom of God**, Jesus displayed his commitment to spreading its message and fulfilling its purpose. This act of submission marked the beginning of his ministry, where he passionately preached about the kingdom, emphasizing its transformative power and calling others to seek it as well. Through his actions, Jesus exemplified the importance of recognizing and submitting to divine authority to carry out one's mission effectively.

Luke 4:43 But he said. "I must preach (the good news of) the Kingdom of God to the other cities also because I was sent for this purpose."

Matthew 5:3 Blessed (happy, to be envied, and spiritually prosperous-with life-joy and satisfaction in God's favor and salvation, regardless of their outward conditions) are the poor in spirit **(the humble, who rate themselves insignificant),** for theirs is the **Kingdom of Heaven!**

The **Kingdom Message** is the only message that can satisfy the **spiritual hunger of human beings**; people are not looking for religion. Religion does not meet the human spirit or the spiritual need.

Only the **Kingdom of God** can do that. If you are spiritually poor, the only thing that can satisfy you is the **Kingdom of God**. Because man's search is for something he lost, not religion; it is his relationship with God, and the **Kingdom Message** reveals man's original purpose for existence.

Every day, man is trying to solve a problem that man created in the first place. The **Kingdom Message** is the answer to all humanity's problems. When the **Kingdom Message** is tested, then the end of all humanity issues will end.

The answers/solutions are in the **Kingdom of God**.

Matthew 24:14 This good news of the kingdom **(the gospel)** will be preached throughout the world as a testimony to all the nations, and then the end **(of the age)** will come.

We must first seek the **Kingdom of God** and His Righteousness, pursue it, study, explore, understand, learn, consider, have a desire to know about it, and have a passion for the **Kingdom of God** and His Righteousness.

Luke 16:16 The Law and the **(writings of the)** prophets were proclaimed until John; since then, the gospel of the **Kingdom of God** has been and continues to be preached, and everyone has tried forcefully to go into it.

After John the Baptist, the only message that should be preached is the **Kingdom of God**; the law was given, and Jesus fulfilled the law; the message is the **Kingdom of God,**

"The Good News." Seeking the **Kingdom of God** reveals who we are as God's creation and our original purpose for existence to have dominion over the things on the earth, not each other.

Gen.1:26 Then God said, "Let us make mankind in our image, in our likeness, so that they may rule over the fish in the sea and the birds in the sky, over the livestock and all the wild animals,[a] and over all the creatures that move along the ground."

The key word here is rule/dominion over; notice not each other but the things on the earth.

Luke 9:11 But when the crowds learned of it, they followed Him; and he welcomed them, and he began talking to them about the **Kingdom of God,** and healing those who needed to be healed.

Matthew 16:19 I will give you the keys **(authority)** of the kingdom of heaven; and whatever you bind **(forbid, declare to be improper and unlawful)** on earth will have **(already)** been bound in heaven, and whatever you loose **(permit, declare lawful)** on earth will have **(already)** been loosed in heaven".

As believers, we have the keys **(principals)** to heaven, the **Kingdom Message. God's Ultimate Divine Vision and Goal** was to rule the earth from heaven through humanity, to **colonize (come to settle among and establish control over)** the earth's territory with the **kingdom of heaven.** We must learn how to pray the will of our Father in heaven into the earth's rim, the standards, principles, and culture of the **Kingdom of Heaven.**

Matthew 6:9 Pray, then, in this way: "Our Father who is in heaven, hallowed be your name. **10:** Your Kingdom comes; your will be done on earth as it is in heaven."

What is The Kingdom of God?

The **Kingdom of God** is referenced throughout the gospels. The Lord Jesus referred to the **Kingdom of God** as the focus of his assignment while here on earth. Repentance is the only way we can inherit this kingdom: a change of heart/mindset, understanding the **Kingdom's Message,** the **"Good News."**

Mark 1:15 And saying, the **(appointed period of)** time is fulfilled **(completed),** and the **Kingdom of God** is at hand; repent **(have a change of mind which issues in regret for past sins and in change of conduct for the better)** and believe **(trust in, rely on, and adhere to)** the good news **(the gospel).**

Mark 10:15 Truly I tell you, whoever does not receive and accept and welcome **the Kingdom of God** like a little child **(does)** positively shall not enter it at all.

Luke 17:20 Once, on being asked by the Pharisees when the Kingdom of God would come, Jesus replied, "The coming of **the Kingdom of God** is not something that can be observed,

[21] nor will people say, 'Here it is,' or 'There it is,' **because the Kingdom of God is in your midst**.

Matthew 13:11 Jesus replied to them, "To you it has been granted to know the mysteries of the Kingdom of heaven, but to them it has not been granted."

This verse of scripture reveals to us that those who will receive the **Kingdom Message** will begin to understand it, and more will be revealed, but those who reject the **Kingdom Message** will not understand it at all.

John 18:36 Jesus answered, **My Kingdom (kingship, royal power)** belongs not to this world. If **My Kingdom** were of this world, my followers would have been fighting to keep me from being handed over to the Jews. But as it is, **My Kingdom** is not from here **(this world).**

Jesus said **His Kingdom** was not of this world and preached that repentance **(change)** is necessary to be a part of the **Kingdom of God.**

Matthew 4:17 From that time, Jesus began to preach, crying out, Repent **(change your mind for the better, heartily amend your ways, with abhorrence of your past sins),** for the **kingdom of heaven** is at hand.

The **Kingdom of God** is the rule of an eternal, sovereign God over the entire universe. **It dwells in the heart of humankind,** those who will receive and believe in the **Kingdom Message** and accept Jesus as savior; he opens the door for us to enter the **Kingdom of God.**

John 14:6 Jesus answered, I am the Way and the Truth and the Life; no one comes to the Father except by (through) Me.

Psalm 103:19 The Lord has established His throne in the heavens, and **His Kingdom** rules over all.

Romans 14:17 (After all), the Kingdom of God is not a matter of **(getting the)** food and drink **(one likes),** but instead it is righteousness **(that state which makes a person acceptable to God)** and **(heart)** peace and joy in the Holy Spirit.

1 Corinthians 15:50 But I tell you, this brethren, flesh, and blood cannot **(become partakers of eternal salvation and)** inherit or share in the **Kingdom of God**; nor does the perishable **(that which is decaying)** inherit or share in the imperishable **(the immortal).**

King Nebuchadnezzar declared, "**His Kingdom** is an eternal Kingdom."

Daniel 4:3 How great are His signs! And how mighty His wonders! **His kingdom** is an everlasting Kingdom, and His dominion is from generation to generation.

Every authority that exists has been established by God. The **Kingdom of God** incorporates everything that is. The **Kingdom of God** is a **spiritual rule over the hearts** and lives of those who willingly submit to God's authority.

Romans 13:1 LET EVERY person be loyally subject to the governing **(civil)** authorities. For there is no authority except from God **(by His permission, His sanction),** and those that exist do so by God's appointment.

What Is

"The Gospel of the Kingdom"

Gospel means **"Good News."** Kingdom is the Greek word **Basileia,** which means **"the realm in which a sovereign king rules."** Throughout the gospel, the word kingdom is being used. When Jesus began His three-year earthly ministry, he preached that **"The Kingdom of Heaven is at hand."**

Mark 1:14 Now, after John was arrested and put in prison, Jesus came into Galilee, preaching the good news **(the gospel)** of the **Kingdom of God.**

15: And saying, the **(appointed period of)** time is fulfilled **(completed),** and the **Kingdom of God** is at hand; repent **(have a change of mind which issues in regret of past sins and a change of conduct for the better)** and believe **trust in, rely on, and adhere to)** the good news **(the gospel).**

The primary reason Jesus came was to preach the **"Good News"** of the **Kingdom of God** when asked to describe it.

Luke 17:20 Asked by the Pharisees when the Kingdom of God would come, he replied to them by saying, the **Kingdom of God** does not come with signs to be observed or with visible display,

21: Nor will people say, Look! Here **(it is)** or see, **(it is)** there! For behold, the **Kingdom of God** is within you **(in your hearts)** and among you **(surrounding you).**

The **Kingdom of God** is **"of righteousness and peace and joy in the Holy Spirit."** Those who receive the Gospel of the Kingdom become citizens of heaven. The **Kingdom of God** frees us from the bondage of this world.

Galatians 4:3 So also, we **(whether Jews or Gentiles),** when we were children **(spiritually immature),** were kept like slaves under the elementary **(man-made religious or philosophical)** teachings of the world.

4: But when **(in God's plan)** the proper time had fully come, God sent His Son, born of a woman, born under the **(regulations of the)** law, ·

5: So that He might redeem and liberate those who were under the law, that we **(who believe)** might be adopted as sons **(as God's children with all rights as fully grown members of a family).**

6: And because you **(really)** are **(His)** sons, God has sent the Spirit of His Son into our hearts, crying out, "Abba! Father!"

7: Therefore, you are no longer a slave **(bondservant),** but a son; and if a son, then also an heir through **(the gracious act of)** God **(through)** Christ.

8: But at that time, when you did not know **(the true)** God and were unacquainted with Him, you **(Gentiles)** were slaves to those **(pagan)** things which by **(their very)** nature were not and could not be gods at all.

9: Now, however, since you have come to know **(the true)** God **(through personal experience),** or rather to be known by God, how is it that you are turning back again to the weak and worthless elemental principles **(of religions and philosophies),** to which you want to be enslaved all over again?

2 Corinthians 5:20 So we are ambassadors for Christ, as though God were making His appeal through us; we **(as Christ's representatives)** plead with you on behalf of Christ to be reconciled to God.

We are **"ambassadors"** for our heavenly Father. Just as an earthly foreign ambassador retains his national identity when representing his country in another, the spiritual ambassadors of **God's Kingdom** owe their allegiance to God even as they reside in this world.

We must learn to follow our heavenly Father's code of conduct on earth and not conform to this world's habits, values, and lifestyle because this is not our home.

Romans 12:1 Therefore I urge you, brothers, and sisters, by the mercies of God, to present your bodies **(dedicating all of yourselves, set apart)** as a living sacrifice, holy and well-pleasing to God, which is your rational **(logical, intelligent)** act of worship.

2: And do not be conformed to this world **(any longer with its superficial values and customs),** but be transformed and progressively changed **(as you mature spiritually)** by the renewing of your mind **(focusing on godly values and ethical attitudes),** so that you may prove **(for yourselves)** what the will of God is, that which is good and acceptable and perfect **(in His plan and purpose for you).**

1 John 2:15 Do not love the world **(of sin that opposes God and His precepts),** nor the things that are in the world. If anyone loves the world, the love of the Father is not in him.

16: For all that is in the world-the lust and sensual craving of the flesh and the lust and longing of the eyes and the boastful pride of life **(pretentious confidence in one's resources or the stability of earthly things)**-these do not come from the Father but are from the world.

17: The world is passing away, and with it its lusts **(the shameful pursuits and ungodly longings),** but the one who does the will of God and carries out His purpose's lives forever.

Although we must live here until God calls us home, we should not live for ourselves or according to this world's value system.

Those whom the blood of Jesus has bought have been given the right to live according to God's value system.

Citizens of the **Kingdom of God** live here on assignment from our Father in heaven. Living with a Kingdom mindset empowers us to make wiser decisions as we invest our lives in furthering the gospel of the kingdom.

God has promised to provide for His own, supplying every need according to His riches in glory in Christ Jesus; as ambassadors of the kingdom, we are commanded to seek first the **Kingdom of God** and His righteousness.

Philippians 4:19 And my God will liberally supply **(fill until full)** your every need according to His riches in glory in Christ Jesus.

Matthews 6:33 But first and most importantly seek **(aim at, strive after) His Kingdom** and His righteousness **(His way**

of doing and being right-the attitude and character of God), and all these things will be given to you also.

34: "So do no worry about tomorrow; for tomorrow will worry about itself. Each day has enough trouble of its own."

The Power of Wisdom

God asked a man named King Solomon, "What do you want most?" and his answer was **"Wisdom."**

Every created being on earth, I genuinely believe, should seek after wisdom. **Wisdom** is the application of knowledge, information that you understand, and "comprehension."

The Lord Jesus came to redeem humanity back to the **Kingdom of God** by obedience to the Word of God until death. This was his purpose and assignment as a human being on earth.

Philippians 2:8 After He was found in **(terms of His)** outward appearance as a man **(for a divinely appointed time),** He humbled Himself **(still further)** by becoming obedient **(to the Father)** to the point of death, even death on a cross.

Jesus had disciples, students, and learners whom he taught the **Kingdom of God** and then told them to do the same. In other words, the application of everything they had learned was **"Wisdom."**

Proverbs 4:5: Get skillful and godly **wisdom**, get understanding **(discernment, comprehension, and interpretation);** do not forget and do not turn back from the words of my mouth.

6: For sake not **(Wisdom),** and she will keep, defend, and protect you; lover her, and she will guard you. **7:** The beginning of **wisdom** is to get **wisdom (skillful and Godly wisdom) (for skillful and Godly Wisdom is the principal thing).** And with all you have gotten, get understanding **(discernment, comprehension, and interpretation).**

Proverbs 24:3 Through skillful and **Godly Wisdom** is a house **(a life, a home, a family)** built, and by understanding, it is established **(on a sound and good foundation).**

4: And by knowledge shall its chambers **(of every area)** be filled with all precious and pleasant riches. **5:** A wise man is strong and is better than a strong man, and a man of knowledge increases and strengthens his power.

James 1:5 If any of you lacks wisdom **(to guide him through a decision or circumstance),** he is to ask of **(our benevolent)** God, who gives to everyone generously and without rebuke or blame, which will be given to him.

6: But he must ask **(for wisdom)** in faith, without doubting **(God's willingness to help),** for the one who doubts is like a billowing surge of the sea that is blown about and tossed by the wind.

7: For such a person ought not to think or expect that he will receive anything **(at all)** from the Lord,

8: Being a double-minded man, unstable and restless in all his ways **(in everything he thinks, feels, or decides).**

The dictionary defines **wisdom** as **"the right use or exercise of knowledge"** and **"the ability to discern or judge what is true, right, or lasting."**

Conversely, knowledge is **"information gained through experience, reasoning, or acquaintance."**

Knowledge can exist without **wisdom,** but not the other way around. One can be knowledgeable without being wise. Knowledge is knowing how to use a gun; **wisdom** is knowing when to use it.

God wants us to have knowledge of the **Kingdom of God** and what He expects of us in His Kingdom. To obey Him, we must know his commands. But as equally important as having knowledge is having **wisdom.** Knowing facts about the Word of God and Scripture is not all there is to **wisdom.**

Wisdom is a gift from God. God blesses us with **wisdom** to glorify Him and use our knowledge of the **Kingdom of God.** The book of Proverbs is the best place in the scriptures to learn of **Godly Wisdom.**

Proverbs 1:7 The reverent and worshipful fear of the Lord is the beginning and the principal and choice part of knowledge **(its starting point and its essence). Still,** fools despise skillful and **Godly Wisdom**, instruction, and discipline.

Knowledge is what is gathered over time through the study of the scriptures. **Wisdom** is the fitting application of **knowledge. Knowledge** understands the light has turned red; **wisdom** applies the breaks. **Knowledge** sees the quicksand: **wisdom** walks around it. **Knowledge** memorizes scripture; **wisdom** obeys them. **Knowledge** learns of God and his Kingdom; **wisdom** loves him.

Wisdom is the proper use of knowledge or information. To know is not to be wise. Many men know a great deal, but some are the greater fool for it. There is no fool so great a fool as a knowing fool. But to understand how to use knowledge is to have **wisdom**.

The dictionary defines **knowledge** as **"facts, information, and skill acquired by a person through experience or education."**

Discipleship is an excellent part of acquiring **knowledge** of the **Kingdom of God** from a teacher of the scriptures **(Jesus, Holy Spirit).**

2 Timothy 3:16 Every scripture is God-breathed **(given by His inspiration)** and profitable for instruction, for reproof and conviction of sin, for correction of error and discipline in obedience, **(and)** for training in righteousness **(in holy living, in conformity to God's will in thought, purpose, and action),**

17: So that the man of God may be complete and proficient, well fitted and thoroughly equipped for every good work.

The Apostle Paul tells Timothy that the Holy Scriptures prepare God's people to be **"thoroughly equipped for every good work."** That includes not only what we do on Sunday but what we do at our offices, in our homes, and in our communities throughout the rest of the week.

Proverbs 18:15 The mind of a prudent **(always)** acquires **knowledge,** and the ear of the wise **(always)** seeks **knowledge.**

Those with understanding can extract the meaning of information. They **"see through"** the facts to the dynamics of what, how, and why. Understanding is a lens that brings the facts into crisp focus and produces principles.

Knowledge: Information, Facts, Memory

Understanding: Meaning, Principles, Reason

Wisdom: What to do next, Application, Action

In any situation, God rarely gives all three gifts to one person. We must cooperate and assist each other with our gift to accomplish what God has called us to do in the **Kingdom of God**, especially in our vocational work.

Ephesians 4:1 I therefore, the prisoner for the Lord, appeal to and beg you to walk **(lead a life)** worth of the **(divine)** calling to which you have been called **(with behavior that is a credit to the summons to God's service,**

2: Living as becomes you) with complete lowliness of mind **(humility)** and meekness **(unselfishness, gentleness, mildness),** with patience, bearing with one another and making allowances because you love one another.

No one person or group of people can have absolute **knowledge** or know all the facts. However, we are all supposed to work towards developing and acquiring **knowledge, wisdom,** and **understanding** in our lives. God is the only one who does not have a **knowledge** problem.

Proverbs 4:5: Get skillful and **Godly wisdom**, get understanding **(discernment, comprehension, and**

interpretation); do not forget and do not turn back from the words of my mouth.

Discernment, in its simplest definition, is nothing more than the ability to decide between truth and error, right and wrong. **Discernment** is the process of making careful distinctions in our thinking about truth. In other words, the ability to think with **discernment** is synonymous with an ability to think Kingdom-minded based on scripture. **Discernment** is the ability to think **Kingdom-minded** about all areas of life; without it, believers are at risk of being **"tossed here and there by waves and carried about by every wind of doctrine."**

Ephesian 4:14 So that we are no longer children **(spiritually immature),** tossed back and forth **(like ships on a stormy sea)** and carried about by every wind of **(shifting)** doctrine, by the cunning and trickery of **(unscrupulous)** men, by the deceitful scheming of people ready to do anything **(for personal profit).**

15: But speaking the truth in love **(in all things - both our speech and our lives expressing His truth),** let us grow up in all things into Him **(following His example)** who is the Head-Christ.

16: From Him the whole body **(the Church, in all its various parts),** joined and knitted firmly together by what every joint supplies, when each part is working properly, causes the body to grow and mature, building itself up in **(unselfish)** love.

God's word provides us with the needed **discernment** about every issue of life. According to Peter, God **"has granted to**

us everything pertaining to life and godliness, through the true knowledge of Him who called us by his own glory and excellence (2 Peter 1:3). It is through the **"true knowledge of Him,"** that we have been given everything we need to live a Godly life in this fallen world. We have the knowledge of the **Kingdom of God**.

Comprehension is the act or action of grasping with the intellect, understanding, knowledge gained by comprehending, and the capacity of understanding fully.

Interpretation is the action of explaining the meaning of something after comprehending it.

Revelation, on the other hand, is what God reveals to us. There are two spheres of **revelation**: the scriptures **(special revelation)** and nature **(general revelation).** God reveals all through **general revelation** in his creation or through **special revelation** in scripture.

What God reveals in nature can never contradict what he reveals in scripture, and what he reveals in scripture can never contradict what he reveals in nature. He is the author of both forms of **revelation and** gives each to us so that we might be equipped for every good work.

For this knowledge to become a path to wisdom, we must learn how to understand both forms of **revelation** together.

The problem of understanding lies not in God's **revelation** but in man's fallible **interpretation** of that **revelation**.

We must learn from past mistakes believers have made in interpreting **general** and **special revelation** and be reminded that we can make the same kinds of mistakes.

Just because fallible human beings can misinterpret **general** and **special revelation** does not mean God's **revelation** is fallible. It means that we are fallible.

We need to pray daily for the illumination of the Holy Spirit to help us understand his word and **revelation,** applying true knowledge to our lives in our search for wisdom in the Kingdom of God. This does not happen overnight. It is a process.

We need to see that God has given us both forms of **revelation** to be used together in our call to glorify him, serve the common good, and further the Kingdom of God.

The Original

Mandate for Mankind

The more I began seeking the Kingdom of God, the more it became obvious to me that we were created for a purpose, and God gave us an original assignment.

Genesis 1:26 And God said, let us make man in our image, after our likeness: and let them have dominion over the fish of the sea, and over the fowl of the air, and over the cattle, and over all the earth, and over every creeping thing that creepeth upon the earth.

27: So, God created man in his own image, in the image of God created he him; male and female created he them.

28: And God blessed them, and God said unto them, be fruitful, and multiply, and replenish the earth, and subdue it: and have dominion over the fish of the sea, and over the fowl of the air, and over every living thing that moveth upon the earth.

The first command God told Adam was to be **fruitful.**

Fruitful: originally means to be productive, to produce, or to be creative. This answered the question I had about my purpose and why so many people are in debt or struggling financially.

Poverty is not the lack of resources but humanity's lack of creativity. It is when we are not producing or using the creativity that God gave us to produce or when we do not use the creativity that God created within us.

God never gave Adam a table, chair, shoes, or buildings or built anything for him. God hid them in the resources he created and told him to manage, such as trees for the table and chairs, animal skin for his clothes, shoes, dirt, and concrete to build buildings, so poverty is the lack of creativity, not the lack of resources.

There is only one crisis, and that is the crisis of creativity. God created us all with creativity and the resources to be creative in the need of a crisis. Money is attracted to creativity; crisis creates creativity and innovation when we recognize a need for something.

Creativity: the use of the imagination or original ideas.

Innovation: the introduction of something new, a new idea, a new method, idea, or product.

God created us and commanded us to be **fruitful (productive).**

When a crisis arises, humankind uses its creativity and innovation to create something new **(product),** good or bad *(principles which will be discussed later).*

The second command God told Adam was to **multiply.** Every successful/wealthy human being on this planet has used this principle, good or bad, to become successful.

For example, McDonald's/Burger King's multi-billion-dollar industry owners have the same burgers worldwide (product), the Big Mac/Whopper; they produce over a billion burgers a month worldwide.

God's 1st command to humankind was to be **fruitful (productive);** they have a product. Because they have applied this God-given principle, their burger businesses are multiplying worldwide and reproducing themselves (principle); everywhere we go today, we can get a Big Mac or Whopper.

The third command God gave humankind was to **replenish** the earth, which means to **distribute**; notice these terms are business terms because the Church is in the business of winning souls for **the Kingdom of God** or redeeming humanity back to his original purpose.

Our original purpose was to be productive **(fruitful)** and multiply **(reproduce). N**ow he says to **distribute (replenish)** the earth, so when you have a useful product, to distribute the product, you need a distribution center **(Church)** to keep the inventory from going bad.

A good businessperson or manager will not let his inventory go bad or keep dead inventory. We need to be reproducing and multiplying the Church **(Body of Christ)** all over the world. Not the building but the product which God created in the beginning.

Lastly, the fourth command was to **subdue** the earth, which means to **control the market,** our product should dominate the market, to take total control over **"dominion."** When we connect ourselves back to our original mandate, which God instructed us to do in the beginning, success is guaranteed.

The question I ask myself daily is what I am doing with the time I have with the gift God gave me. I have come to realize that my life is a gift from God, ready to **produce fruit, reproduce, multiply, replenish,** and **subdue the earth.**

So, **domination** or **dominion (controlling the market)** is not a pursuit; it is the result of following God's original mandate for humanity, the Kingdom agenda **(dominion).**

God's Original Plan was to extend his invisible Kingdom/Heaven on earth through humankind, influencing earth from heaven through the rulership of His children on earth, establishing a colony of heaven on earth, colonizing Earth with Heaven, filling the earth with His glory, nature, and culture.

The Kingdom of God Influences us to Influence Others.

To **dominate** does not mean **dominating** people but being **influential** with your purpose/gift. God created us to be an **influence** on earth. Most people die and never **influence** anyone in their neighborhood, community, or family with the **Kingdom of God**. The **Kingdom Message** will empower, encourage, and motivate us to be what God created us to be.

Influential means having a great **influence** on someone or something. **Influence** means the capacity to have an effect on the character, development, or behavior of someone or something.

Dominating in life, the area of life where God has a place of purpose, by effectively communicating your purpose in life by impacting God's will on earth. Whoever **dominates** in areas of life will have an **influence** on earth, which will **influence** others to do the same.

The effects of **influential** people last forever, even after they die, but famous people eventually go away unless they are **influential.**

After seeking the Kingdom of God, I have discovered we were placed in time/born to **influence** a generation.

God placed us in a body not to be popular but to be **influential** to a generation of people once we understand the **Kingdom of God's** agenda.

Matthew 13:33 He told another parable: The **Kingdom of Heaven** is like leaven **(sourdough)** which a woman took and covered over in three measures of meal or flour till all of it was leavened.

Dough, yeast means making a difference, impacting, or being influential in our world.

Matthew 5:13 You are the salt of the earth, but if salt has lost its taste **(its strength, its quality)**, how can its salt-ness be restored? It is not good for anything any longer but to be thrown out and trodden underfoot by men.

14: You are the light of the world. A city set on a hill cannot be hidden.

We are the salt of the earth, flavor, season; when you season something, it preserves and makes it better. We are the light of the world; when we show up, God is there; we impact the dark, influence the dark, and bring light to dark places.

Matthew 13:44 The Kingdom of Heaven is like something precious buried in a field, which a man found and hid again; then in his joy he goes and sells all he has and buys that field.

The **Kingdom of Heaven** is a state of mind **(Kingdom Mindset).** The kingdom is like a treasure, something valuable that was lost **(what humankind lost);** it is precious, and when we find it, it becomes valuable. Once found, we become willing to give up or sacrifice everything we have for it; when looking or searching for something hidden in a field **(treasure),** it takes work, precision, or digging to find it.

The scripture said that when he found it, he sold all he had and bought the entire field. He could have just taken the treasure, but he was willing to give up everything he had to take on the responsibility of the entire field. Finding something valuable takes sacrifice and hard work.

Once we accomplish the search and find the treasure/the **Kingdom of God**, there is no need to look no more for things. But the question is what we are willing to sacrifice or give up for the Kingdom of God once we discover it.

No one knew about the treasure he found, but he hid it again from himself and took on the responsibility of owning the whole field.

The kingdom is precious, so he will not lose it again; he takes on the responsibility of owning the entire field. When we take on ownership and responsibilities, the chances of losing something again are slim.

The **Kingdom of God** is about understanding what humankind lost **(relationship, fellowship with God)** and the responsibilities that God gave humankind in the beginning **to manage** the things on the earth **(field).**

That is why the Lord Jesus said to seek first the **Kingdom of God** and His righteousness; the more we seek it, our purpose and destiny will be revealed.

The purpose of Jesus was to reveal the **Kingdom of God** and redeem us back to our original mandate/purpose and glorify our Father, which is in heaven, by declaring the **Kingdom of God** is here, and those who accept the **Kingdom Message** and repent of their sins will be saved from the world system.

There is nothing new; the Lord's plan remains the same. The **Kingdom Message** reveals that.

Ecclesiastes 1:9 Things that has been it is what will be again, and that which has been done is that which will be done again, and there is **nothing new under the sun.**

10: Is there a thing of which it may be said, see, this new? It has already been, in the vast ages of time **(recorded or unrecorded)** which were before us.

11: There is no remembrance of former happenings or men, neither will there be any remembrance of happenings of generations that are to come by those who are to come after them.

Jesus died for our past sins, forgave and forgot them, and redeems our future. Once we repent and become a part of the **Kingdom of God**, continue to seek the **Kingdom of God** until he returns.

Job 8:5 If you will seek God diligently and make your supplication to the Almighty,

6: Then, if you are pure and upright, surely, He will bestir Himself for you and make your righteous dwelling prosperous again.

Psalm 37:3 Trust **(lean on, rely on, and be confident)** in the Lord and do good: so, shall you dwell in the land and feed surely on His faithfulness, and truly you shall be fed.

4: Delight yourself in the Lord, and he will give you the desires and secret petition of your heart.

5: Commit your way to the Lord **(roll and repose each care of your load on Him)**; trust **(lean on, rely on, and be confident)** also in Him, and He will bring it to pass.

The future gives hope to the past; leave the past behind and press on. God has forgiven us and forgotten our sins.

Philippians 3:12 Not that I have now attained (**this deal**), or have already been made perfect, but I press on to lay hold of (**grasp**) and make my own, that for which Christ Jesus (**the Messiah**) has laid hold of me and made me His own.

13: I do not consider, brethren, that I have captured and made it my own (**yet**); but one thing I do (**it is my one aspiration**); forgetting what lies behind and straining forward to what lies ahead,

14: I press toward the goal of winning the (**supreme and heavenly**) prize to which God in Christ Jesus is calling us upward.

Our future is more important than our past; learn from the past, close the door, and move forward in the **Kingdom of God.** Life is a marathon, not a sprint. I have learned to use time wisely because every day, we have an opportunity to fulfill the purpose of God on earth.

Ecclesiastes 9:11 I returned and saw under the sun that the race is not to the swift nor the battle to the strong neither is bread to the wise nor riches to men of intelligence and understanding nor favor to men of skill, but time and chance happen to them all.

12: For man also knows not his time (**of death**): as the fishes are taken in an evil net, and as the birds are caught in the snare, so are the sons of men snared in an evil time when (**calamity**) falls suddenly upon them.

13: This (**illustration of**) wisdom have I seen also under the sun, and it seemed great to me.

Prioritizing Our Time

Matthew 6:33 But first and most importantly seek (**aim at, strive after**) His Kingdom and His righteousness (**His way of doing and being right-the attitude and character of God),** and all things will be given to you also.

"Whatever is most important to us is our driving force; it becomes our priority."

Priority means the principal thing, putting first things first, establishing the most important thing, the primary focus, placing in order of importance, placing the highest value and worth upon something important, first among all others.

The Divine Command of Jesus is to **seek** the **Kingdom of God** and His Righteousness 1st. **Seek** means to pursue study, explore, understand, learn, consider, and desire to know, have a passion, diligent dedication, and preoccupy oneself with the **Kingdom of God**.

First means priority, principle, before all others, the most important, highest value, above everything. Jesus has informed us we do not have to seek things or even pray for things if we have our priorities straight.

In fact, in that chapter, he says when we pray, pray for the kingdom to come and the will of God to be done on earth as it is in heaven.

Matthew 6:9 Pray, therefore, like this: Our Father Who is in heaven, hallowed (kept holy) be Your name.

10: Your Kingdom comes; your will be done on earth as it is in heaven.

The Kingdom of God

God's government, rulership, dominion over the earth, will, heavenly influence, administration, and impact on the earth, righteousness, right positioning with God, being in alignment with his word and authority, being in fellowship with God, being in correct standing with the Word of God (**His Principles**).

When we are in right standing with God and His Word, we become Royal Priest, Sons of God, Citizens of the Kingdom of God. We are Royal Priesthood Sons of the Most High God, Our Father in Heaven, and we have the authority to dominate the things on the earth, not each other.

Maslow's Theory of Behavioral Science States Man's 1st Interest of Priority is:

1: Water to Drink

2: Food to Eat

3: Clothes to cover our Body (flesh)

4: Housing to live in and put things in furniture, etc.

5: Protection to protect the things we have

6: Security to keep others from taking the things we have

7: Preservation to preserve or store up the things we have

8: Self Actualization to use the things we have

Maslow survey of humanity covers all humans, regardless of nationality, culture, or creed; this is what we seek as human beings every day. In fact, some would even do anything for these things to survive here on earth.

According to the divine command of our Lord and Savior Jesus Christ **(God Himself),** there are two main priorities in life we should seek first, and all those things we need will be given to us: **"The Kingdom of God & His Righteousness"** he does not say seek after things.

The Two Powers of Life we can never control or stop are **time** and **change**. The two most difficult components in life to manage are **time** and **change.**

We become who we are because we use **time** and manage the **changes** in our lives. I have realized that the key to our future is the successful management of **time** and **change;** we cannot stop either. All we can do is manage them; every day, week, month, and year is a gift God gives us to fulfill our purpose in life.

We were born and placed in a body to complete a task and fulfill a purpose established by God. We do not have forever to fulfill our earthly purpose. What we do with our **time** is so important because our time is limited.

Job 14:5 Since a man's days are already determined and the number of his months is in your control, and he cannot pass the bounds of his allotted time.

We have a limited **time** to fulfill or accomplish God's purpose, so we must learn to prioritize our **time** and manage the **changes** in our lives.

Time is the measured or measurable period during which an action, process, or condition exists or continues, a moment, hour, day, or year as indicated by a clock or calendar, the period during which something is used or available for use.

1. Success in life is based on the way we use our time; time is the true measure of life.
2. Success in life is the effective use of time.
3. How we spend our time determines the quality of our life.
4. Whatever we spend our time on the most is what we will become.
5. Whatever or whoever controls our time controls our life.
6. If we do not identify our priorities in life, people or things will.
7. Everything and everyone is after our time.
8. The key to the correct use of time is the correct priorities of our time.

Why is it Important to Change our Minds?

We are the only creatures on this earth that can decide to change. The animal world lives on instincts; we will never find animals sitting down planning change, a group of sharks or fish meeting together, planning to change, or deciding their future.

I have never seen a group of trees congregating together, deciding how they will change.

We are the only creatures on the planet that can sit down and plan the kind of future or life we want.

Changing our thinking, mind, will, and the power of will is the most powerful gift God ever gave man.

The power of choice: we can choose to serve God or be against God. The will of man is so powerful man can tell his creator, the one who gave him life, that he does not even exist.

Powerful, huh? WOW!!!

There are people somewhere right now in a closed room deciding the future policy and the direction of this country, government, state, city, and the entire world, and some of us are not there.

We are victims of other people's decisions and their will as a people, community, and society.

But a lot of folks will not even vote; some will not even try to better understand the **Kingdom of God** and its policies or God's will for our lives, His governmental authority, and His direction for our lives as **Kingdom Citizens** and seek **His righteousness** to fulfill His will and purpose in the earth.

That is why getting knowledge and the Wisdom of God is so important. The principal thing to get is wisdom, and with all thy getting, gain an understanding.

Proverbs 4:7 Wisdom is the principal thing; therefore, get wisdom: and with all thy getting get understanding.

As we continue to seek after the **Kingdom of God** and understand it, the **"Wisdom"** of the **Kingdom of God** can empower, encourage, and inspire this world we live in, the principles and values of the power of the **Gospel Message**.

The **Kingdom of God** is the message we, as believers, are called to declare to all nations; this is the message that Jesus preached and taught to his disciples.

They preached the reality of the **Kingdom of God**, the authority of the **Kingdom of God**, the Power of the **Kingdom of God,** and the Concepts of the **Kingdom of God**.

It is important to understand why Jesus came to redeem mankind back to God, back to our original purpose and mandate to be in fellowship with our creator.

The more we seek the **Kingdom of God** and **His righteousness, the more** we will begin to discover what we should be, and what we will learn about ourselves is what we will become.

We must change our thinking if we are not what or where we want to be. That is why it is essential to change our thinking, develop the right attitude about ourselves, see how God sees us, and **change** our perception of who we are as God's children. Once we discover our purpose, we can become our purpose.

Proverbs 23:7 For as he thinks in his heart, so is he.

In other words, we are whatever we think in our hearts. It is essential to **change** our thoughts.

Philippians 2:5 Let this same attitude and purpose and (**humble**) mind be in you which was in Christ Jesus: (**let Him be your example in humility**).

Powerful Quotes

1. It is not what you are that holds you back; it is what you think you are not that holds you back.
2. You cannot always change circumstances, but you can always control your thoughts.
3. Nothing changes until your mind changes.
4. The information does not bring transformation; conversion does. **Example:** *People who have been attending Church for years and still have not changed.*

5. Teaching the word brings revelation, but the transfer of spirit brings transformation.

6. As a man thinks in his heart, that is the man; as a man thinks in his heart, so is he.

7. The most difficult project in the world is the reconstruction of the human mind; it is easier to go to Mars than to reconstruct the human mind.

8. You are the sum of all you have been conditioned to think.

9. Belief does not guarantee conviction; just because we believe something does not mean it convicts us. We do not change until conviction takes place. **Example:** *How often have we agreed to something but did not do it? How often have you told yourself it is true but did not convict you enough to cause you to act?*

10. The thinking of the mind changes only when we conceive what we believe and accept what we hear; we do not change until our conception.

11. The most powerful force on earth is the will of man, the power of choice.

12. People are not sent to hell; they decide to go.

13. What we see and hear are small compared to what we think because what we think interprets what we see and hear.

14. The most difficult attempt of God Himself was to try to change the minds of formerly enslaved people; it was easier to deliver them

from the enemy, but to change their minds was difficult.

15. Miracles do not change people or the minds of people.

For example, **Exodus 13:17** So it happened when Pharaoh let the people go, God did not lead them by way of the land of the Philistines, even though it was nearer; for God said, **"The people might change their minds when they see war (that is, that there will be war), and return to Egypt."**

God had delivered these people and performed many miracles, but their attitude and mindset never changed, and most of that generation did not make it to the promises that the Lord promised. These people were in slavery/bondage for over four hundred years; once God had delivered them, a 30-day journey took them over 40 years because of their attitude/mindset.

They were conditioned to slavery, the service industry, and servants; they were accustomed to the slavery/servant mentality. These people could not manage deliverance and were victims of mental and historical conditioning. They accepted their external conditioning as their internal destiny; they decided the way it was on the outside was the way I was on the inside, and they allowed the atmosphere to create their attitude.

They were physically relocated, intellectually motivated, but spiritually paralyzed, so changing location does not alter mentality; you can take people out of Egypt but cannot take Egypt out of the people.

God fed the people manna from heaven and water from rocks; they wore the same clothes and shoes for over 40 years, healed them when sick, and performed miracle after miracle in their lives.

Some people today have food, clothes, shoes, jobs, and money and have been healed. The **"Miracles"** still have not changed them, and they complain.

Good preaching and teaching should **change** the mentality of people, not necessarily make us feel good; the Good News of **The Kingdom of God** changes the mindset of people, and change does not always feel good.

Jesus changed the minds of twelve disciples/men to **change** the world; the actual assignment of the Church, the Kingdom Mandate, the Kingdom Message, and the Original Mandate of Man is to change the mind, mentality, and lifestyle of people back to our original purpose to have a relationship with God.

The Goal of the oppressor/enemy is to keep us ignorant of the truth, a broken spirit. Jesus came to renew our **thinking** or **change** our mindset to free us from the oppressor.

Luke 4:18 The spirit of the Lord is upon me **(the Messiah)** because he has anointed me to preach the good news to the poor. He has sent me to announce the release **(pardon, forgiveness)** to the captives and recovery of sight to the blind, to set free those who are **OPPRESSED (downtrodden, bruised, crushed by tragedy).** 19: to proclaim that favorable year of the Lord

(the day when salvation and the favor of God abound greatly).

I heard this story about the power of conditioning; some scientists wanted to test it.

They brought out this beautiful dog, chained him up, and had the chains at a certain length, and they put some fresh meat out. They put the meat out and place it just beyond the chain length.

The dog would run towards the meat, and just before he got to the meat, the chain would yank him back. Every day they did this, fresh meat and the dog would run and yank himself back, sometimes even hurt him.

They did this for a couple of weeks. After a couple of weeks of doing this, one day, the dog just sat there and looked at the meat; the next day, they came out, took the chains off the dog, and put the meat out, the dog just looked at the meat he stayed by the stake and just looked at it.

They pushed the meat closer to the dog; he backed away from the meat and just looked at it. He was free.

But he had been conditioned; in other words, when we are conditioned to think a certain way for a long time or think like a slave or be oppressed all our lives, even after we are set free, or doors are open, we will stay in the prison of our minds.

Jesus came to preach the **"Good News,"** announcing release, pardon, and freedom to the captive; he declared the doors open to those in prison or oppressed.

We are God's children **(King Kids)**. We must learn to condition our minds to think **Kingdom Minded** like God's Kids **(Royal Priest).**

Prince Charles was trained as a child to think, act, dress, and have a separate set of values. He was groomed from a child to be a King **(Royalty).**

That is the assignment of true ministry to tutor, mentor, and remind people of whom we belong to and who we really are as **Kingdom Citizens** and representatives of the **Kingdom of God.**

But the question is? Is it possible to change our minds in this lifetime and discover the gift of leadership within as a **Kingdom Citizen** and empower this world we live in with the gifts given to us?

Roman 12:2 Do not be conformed to this world **(this age), (fashioned after and adapted to its external, superficial customs)**, but be transformed **(changed)** by the **(entire)** renewal of your mind **(by its new ideas and its new attitude),** so that you may prove **(for yourselves)** what is the good and acceptable and perfect will of God, even the things which are good and acceptable and perfect **(in His sight for you).**

The most powerful forces on earth are **Change** and **Time** because **Change** and **Time** are guaranteed.

Genesis 8:22 While the earth remains, seedtime and harvest, cold and heat, summer and winter, and day night shall not cease.

Daniel 2:20 Daniel answered, blessed be the name of God forever and ever! For wisdom and might are His!

21: He **changes** the **times** and the seasons; he removes kings and sets up kings. He gives wisdom to the wise and knowledge to those who have understanding!

Wisdom and power belong to God. God has the power to **change** things and the wisdom or insight to **change** things, so in other words, God will initiate **Change** and **Time.**

Ecclesiastes 3:1 to everything, there is a season and a time for every matter or purpose under heaven.

2: a time to be born and time to die, a time to plant and a time to pluck up what is planted.

God has the power over seasons in His **Time;** all we can do is manage **Time** and **Change.**

Why Because:

1. Seasons guarantee change.
2. Seasons give hope.
3. Nothing remains the same.
4. Seasons are always temporary.
5. Seasons give you the incentive to plan.
6. Seasons are always moving.
7. The key to life is outlasting seasons.
8. Never respond permanently to a temporary problem.

Four Types of Changes in Our Life

1. Change that happens to us.

2.   Change that happens around us.
3.   Change that happens within us.
4.   Change that we make happen.

But change comes with choices; we must choose to change.

Discovering

The Leader Within

Leadership is like a tree trapped in a seed; for the seed to grow into a tree requires the right environment. Seed grows according to its environment.

Example: If you plant a seed in a pot in the house but plant that same seed in your yard or a field, it will grow according to the environment.

Everyone is growing into a tree to produce branches and then fruit. The more we abide in the **Kingdom Message,** the words that Jesus taught, the more we will grow.

John 15:1 I am the vine, and My Father is the vinedresser.

2: Every branch in Me that does not bear fruit, he takes away; and every branch that continues to bear fruit, he (**repeatedly**) prunes, so that it will bear more fruit (**even richer and finer fruit**)

3: You are already clean because of the word which I have given you (**the teachings which I have discussed with you**)

4: Remain in me, and I (**will remain**) in you. Just as no branch can bear fruit by itself without remaining in the vine, neither can you (**bear fruit, producing evidence of your faith**) unless you remain in Me.

We were born to grow and produce fruit. There is something on the inside of everyone that no one has seen yet. Everyone is still growing. Our Gift/Purpose is the leadership fruit we lead in our gifting. People are not attracted to us, but they are attracted to our gift: **"I encourage you to serve your fruit."**

Character is the foundation of God's leadership. God's character never changes; it remains the same. God gave us his character when he created us in his image and likeness.

Genesis 1:26 Then God said, "Let us (**Father, son, Holy Spirit**) make man in our image, according to our likeness (**not physical, but a spiritual personality and moral likeness**); and let them have complete authority over the fish of the sea, the birds of the air, the cattle, and over the entire earth, and over everything that creeps and crawls on the earth

27: So, God created man in His own image, in the image and likeness of God he created him; male and female he created them.

28: And God blessed them (**granting them certain authority**) and said to them, "Be fruitful, multiply, and fill the earth, subjugate it (**putting it under your power**); and rule over (**dominate**) the fish of the sea, the birds of the air, and every living thing that moves upon the earth."

This is what we were created to do, to dominate over things on the earth, not people, which takes character, the character of God, the original plan of God, leadership was put in us by God Himself.

Everyone is born to lead, but you must become a leader.

1. Trapped in every follower is a hidden leader.
2. Every human was created to lead and designed for dominion.
3. Leadership potential resides in every individual.
4. The purpose of true leadership is to produce leaders.

Leadership is the capacity to **Influence** others through **Inspiration** generated by a **Passion** motivated by a **Vision** born by a **Conviction** produced by a **Purpose.**

Becoming a leader is to reverse the definition:

Understanding Our Purpose: Original Intent

Conviction: Strong Belief

Vision: Purpose in Picture

Passion: Desire for Change

Inspiration: Encouraging Others

Influence: Submission to a Cause

5 Questions to answer to be a Leader.

1. Who am I **(Identity)**? Once discovered, I got to believe it.
2. Why am I here **(Purpose)** must be discovered/self-discovery.
3. What can I do **(Potential)** Self-Exposure/Expose your purpose/gift?
4. Where am I from **(Heritage)** Kings Child/in the world/not of the world?
5. Where am I going **(Destiny)**? Serve your gift to the world.

Why We Need Leaders

1. Nothing happens without leadership.
2. Nothing begins without leadership.
3. Nothing improves without leadership.
4. Nothing develops without leadership.
5. Nothing changes without leadership.
6. Nothing progresses without leadership.
7. Nothing succeeds without leadership.

True Leadership

1. Leadership is not about control but service.
2. Leadership is not about power but empowerment.

3. Leadership is not about manipulation but inspiration.
4. Leadership is not about people but purpose.

The Greatest Act of Leadership "Mentoring"

Jesus Christ never built a building; he built people. The greatest investment in life is investing in the lives of people. We built buildings to build people; true legacy is in people, not buildings.

If what we learn, achieve, accumulate, or accomplish all die with us, who does it benefit?

A true leader's focus is leading others to leadership. Mentoring is the manifestation of the highest level of maturity and self-confidence.

We need leaders more interested in people than private ambition, and the obligation of true leadership is to transfer your deposit to the next generation.

Leadership is not a sprint but a marathon relay race, passing the Paton to the next generation. We need leaders who are more dedicated to history **(his story)** than they are to money.

The Importance of Planning

James 2:26 For just as the **(human)** body without the spirit is dead, so faith without works **(of obedience)** is also dead.

Hebrews 11:6 But without faith it is impossible to **(walk with God and)** please Him, for whoever comes **(near)** to God must **(necessarily)** believe that God exists and that He rewards those who **(earnestly and diligently)** seek Him.

Planning is the highest level of faith. If you believe something, you plan for it. Faith is the ability to see the unseen in detail and give it substance. To give something substance, you must write it down or draw it out to see it.

Planning is the ability to document the future. God is a God of faith; Planning is the highest expression of our faith in God. Believing God and writing it down shows how much we believe and plan to receive it. When you believe something, you plan for it; you document it.

Planning is an act of capturing God's will for your life. In writing, it defines our faith and pulls the promises of God out of eternity into time and reality.

Planning documents vision; without vision, people perish. A plan captures vision; without a plan, there is no self or goal control.

Faith is our expression of planning; without faith, it is impossible to please God. Faith without works is dead. Faith is expressed in planning; planning is faith.

Many plans have fallen because of lack of work or not following through. Planning is the key to the success of our faith coming to pass or reality. When we believe in God, he wants us to plan; planning without works is a failure.

Psalms 16:9: A man's mind plans his way, but the Lord directs his steps and makes them sure.

So, we make the plan, and God directs us, but how can God guide us without a plan? He knows our plan, but we must work on the plan. The greatest example of planning is in God's Word; all things are possible with God and his plan for our lives. God planned to redeem humanity back to himself through Christ Jesus.

He thought the plan, discussed it, wrote it, made it clear, and placed it in the Heart of Men, fulfilling it through us.

God's plan is awesome. We can learn from God's plan; you cannot change anything if you do not have a plan. Even if your plan fails, it does not mean you are not in the will of God. Failure just allows you to start over again, and we serve a God of a second chance. We only lose when we quit.

When we begin to understand the **Kingdom of God** and its purpose for our lives and begin to write the plan to fulfill that purpose, our plans may change the more God reveals his direction for our lives in the **Kingdom of God.** The principal thing is that principals never change, but our plans may change to fulfill God's purpose.

Proverbs 19:21 Many plans are in a man's mind, but it is the Lord's purpose for him that will stand **(be carried out).**

The Lord commits himself to fulfilling purpose and destiny in our lives. So be encouraged and continue to write because when we write the plan and make it plain and strive each day to fulfill God's purpose for our lives, the God we serve is the God who will be responsible for ordering our steps and bringing that plan to reality.

Experience is our best teacher **(not true).** I have come to find out that when experience becomes our best teacher, it could prevent us from progressing in life or cause us to stop progressing. Because we will find ourselves judging or measuring our dreams and visions by our past experiences:

1. I tried that before.
2. I never seen anyone step out and do it that way.
3. That will never work.

We will begin to allow our experiences to stop us from progressing in life. **(Doubt)** will slip in, and that is the opposite of faith. I believe that's why God always makes history with people not caught up with past experiences, traditionalism, or religion.

I discovered that if you continue to worship your past, you will stay stuck there and never progress in life. God is calling this next generation to do greater works because some people have too much experience, good and bad. And many of our experiences may not necessarily be right, just a lesson we learn.

Example: David and Goliath. The problem with King Sol was he had too much experience; what worked for him could not work for David. He told David to wear his armor, shield, and sword; the young man said, "This is too heavy for me." Some of us can be trying to lay some heavy stuff on the next generation. How we did it, what we did, the mistakes we made, and God is still revealing revelation to this next generation every day.

Today, some of the stuff we did will never work, but David uses a sling and a rock, which had never been done before.

Something the giant never saw or experienced: how do you come to a fight with a rock and slingshot against a trained giant with a sword? The giant expected a trained fighter with a sword and shield to fight him.

But here comes this young man (**David**) from the next generation with this new equipment, something the enemy had never seen before and destroyed him.

The Church needs today some young folk who would come against the enemy with something he is not expected to show up with. Using innovation and creativity, tapping into our original purpose and substances God created us with. Confusing and destroying the enemy.

But thank God for the **Kingdom Message,** which provides us with the comfort of knowing Jesus has already done just that: destroyed the works of the enemy.

1 John 3:8 The one who practices sin (**separating himself from God, and offending Him by acts of disobedience, indifference, or rebellion**) is of the devil (**and takes his inner character and moral values from him, not God**); for the devil has sinned and violated God's law from the beginning. **The Son of God appeared for this purpose, to destroy the works of the devil.**

"I have come to realize in life it is okay to consult with my past experiences, but never let my past experiences rule over me. God is revealing his kingdom to me, but I cannot allow my past experiences to hinder me from progressing because of my past experiences."

God is revealing visions and dreams of the **Kingdom of God,** and some people with past experiences who do not understand the **Kingdom of God** can be discouraged because they do not understand the **Kingdom's Message.**

"God is saying I didn't ask you to consult with people; I just need you to believe me and say yes, then seek ye 1ˢᵗ the Kingdom of God and My Righteousness and everything you need will be supplied, don't worry about the past, old things are passed away." He who worships the past will remain in the past; if we worship the past, we will never progress or move forward in life.

I learned that life's Goal is not to preserve history but to make history. We are the salt **(preserve)** of the earth, so we preserve the earth, not history. True legacy is in people because people carry legacy to the next generation.

So, I encourage you to continue to press toward the mark of the higher calling in Jesus Christ. Our goal in life should not just be reading history but making history. The next generation should be reading about us.

Staying on Course of the Plan

Proverbs 19:21 Many plans are in a man's mind, but it is the Lord's purpose for him that will stand **(be carried out).**

Psalms 57:2 I will cry to God Most High, who performs on my behalf and rewards me **(who brings to pass His purposes for me and surely completes them)!**

God commits himself to fulfill purpose and destiny in our lives.

Psalms 138:8 The Lord will accomplish that which concerns me; your **(unwavering)** lovingkindness, O'Lord, endures forever, do not abandon the works of your own hand.

God will never abandon what he has given us to do.

Ephesians 1:11 In Him also we have received an inheritance **(a destiny-we were claimed by God as His own),** having been predestines **(chosen, appointed beforehand)** according to the purpose of Him who works everything in agreement with the counsel and design of His will.

1. Chose Us.
2. Predestined Us **(Start–End).**
3. Conforms all things to his will **(Good, Bad, Mistakes and Failures).**

Whatever we fail to do, God will use it as a testimony for his purpose to keep us on course. No failure can stop God's destiny for our lives; only we can. God is committed to our destiny; the question is, are we? I believe we must try not to live casually, or we will become casualties of life. It is important to have a plan, follow through, and be faithful to the plan.

It is a privilege to be living **(Gift of God)**. We must learn how to handle life because no position in life places us above counsel **(we can always learn)**. A fool says in his heart he knows all things **(only God knows all things**).

The greatest mistake man can ever make is to believe he can never make one. The ignorance of man is to believe that he knows everything.

The greatest misunderstanding of a man is to believe that he understands everything. All you learn is all you know, or all you know is what you have learned, and all you have learned is not all there is to know. So, no matter what you know, you still do not know some things. The unknown is much larger than the known; in other words, there is a whole lot to know that we do not know.

Psalms 131:1 Lord, my heart is not proud, nor my eyes haughty; nor do I involve myself in great matters or in things too difficult for me.

In other words, I will not exercise myself in matters too high for me. That is why it is so important to choose our chosen destiny, what God has chosen for us.

It is up to us; God does not study or obey himself for us. We must do those things. Staying on course depends on the choices or decisions we make in life.

The route we choose to take determines our destiny based on the decisions we make in life. We can write out a plan or resolution, but we must decide to start doing it to fulfill the plan or resolution. Making plans alone does not always guarantee success. It is the choices we make to stay on course of the plan. That alone will determine our destiny by choosing or deciding to stay on course.

Example: God created all things, and everything God created is good. Everything that God created, He created for a purpose, and understanding the purpose of a thing will allow us to understand how to use a thing or apply it to our lives. When we do not understand the purpose of a thing, we will misuse whatever God created.

Spending all our time watching TV, smoking weed, wasting time, or drinking alcohol will lead to alcoholism. Showing up late for work leads to being fired, sleeping around leads to divorce if married, or transmitting disease. Not eating right, getting enough rest, or exercising can result in bad health conditions. We don't have to get a deep revelation of that; we know the course we have chosen when doing those things. The question is, do we want to stay on that course of life or decide to follow God's course for our life?

Some questions to ask ourselves:

1. Where do I want to go in life?
2. What do I want to achieve in life?
3. What are my heart's desires?
4. Have I set a course for my life?
5. Am I still on course?
6. Is my present course taking me to my destiny?

7. Are the things I am doing presently leading me to my dreams?

8. Have I been detoured from my course?

9. Am I satisfied with the course I am on?

Isaiah 26:3 You will guard him and keep him in perfect and constant peace whose mind **(both its inclination and its character)** is stayed on you because he commits himself to you, leans on you and hopes confidently in you.

4: So, trust in the Lord **(commit yourself to Him, lean on Him, hope confidently in Him)** forever, for the Lord God is an everlasting rock **(the Rock of Ages).**

Psalms 37:4 Delight yourself also in the Lord, and He will give you the desires and secret petition of your heart.

The Power of Vision

Hebrews 11:1 Now faith is the substance of things hoped for, the evidence of things not seen.

(AMPC) Now, faith is the assurance **(the confirmation, the title deed)** of the things **(we)** hope for, being the proof of things **(we)** do not see and the conviction of their reality **(faith perceiving as real fact what is not revealed to the senses).**

Vision is the greatest source of hope…

I believe we can learn from the eagle, the King of the bird Kingdom. It flies at a high altitude. It does not hang with other birds. You will not find the eagle hanging with the pigeons, ducks, swans, or other birds because it flies high in the sky.

Its attitude soars high in the sky, flying and gazing towards the hills from where its help comes. It always presses towards the mark of a higher calling, soaring high in the sky, looking up.

Therefore, if the eagle runs into pigeons, that means it is flying too low, but you will never find the eagle hanging with pigeons. We can tell where we are in life by seeing those people we keep meeting up with or find ourselves hanging around. The eagle does not hang with pigeons, gossipers, murmurers, complainers, or those who always find fault with you or the Church or have the wrong attitude. They will always shift on you.

In other words, you can tell where you are in life by those who you attract in your life. Are you attracting pigeons, complainers, murmurs, and fault-finders? Jesus knew he was stuck with his family, but he chose his friends. He selected his associations based on his destination.

I believe the Lord will allow us to meet or place us around certain people to take us to another level in life to fly higher. God wants to do wonderful things in our lives, but some people will not leave the pack of pigeons.

Eagles do not fly with other birds. The eagle mentality does not mix with complainers, critics, slanders, and murmuring people. Your dreams are bigger than that. If we want to be great, we cannot keep company with gossipers, fault-finders, and doubters; God is bigger than that. Can I encourage you to choose your friends based on your destination?

One of the greatest gifts God has given us is not the gift of sight but the gift of **vision**. Sight is a function of the eyes, and **vision** is the function of the heart. Sight is limited, but **vision** sees beyond your imagination. Your eyes show you what it is, but your **vision** shows what could be. Sight restricts you to the present, and **vision** releases you to your future.

We must be careful about our past because we can become a victim of our past and get caught up in the good old days and not create new ones. We can be caught up in our past and be stuck in the present, thinking about the good old days and not creating new ones.

I heard a story about a 4-year-old girl who went on a cruise with her parents. They were on the top deck looking out, viewing the view, and the little girl was too small to see. So, she started yanking her dad's pants and hitting his leg. "Daddy, I want to see, I want to see."

The Father picked his little girl up and placed her on his shoulders, and this made her so excited. She said, "Daddy, Daddy, look," and he said, "What?", "Daddy look," and he asked again, "What?" She said, **"I CAN SEE FARTHER THAN MY EYES CAN LOOK."** That day, a 4-year-old little girl defined what **VISION** is.

Vision is the capacity to see farther than your eyes can look, so **vision** is the greatest source of hope; we were born to see beyond our eyes because:

Hebrews 11:1 Now faith is the substance of things hoped for, the evidence of things not seen.

God is the Creator of All Things & Heaven is the Manufactory

Genesis 1:1 In the beginning, God (prepared, formed, fashioned, and) created the heavens and the earth.

Psalms 24:1 The Earth is the Lord's and the fullness of it, the world and they who dwell in it.

Every manufacturer creates a product for the purpose of performing something. Mankind is the greatest product that God ever created, and He created mankind for a purpose, and our manufacturer is heaven.

Every product that was ever created on earth first was a thought in someone's mind, and God had humankind on his mind at the beginning of creation.

When a good manufacturer manufactures a product, it comes with a manual or manuscript, which is the mind of the creator of the product.

The creator's intention is for you to read the manual to understand how the product works and how it functions.

If we read and follow the instructions in the manual, the product will perform correctly.

Before the product leaves the manufacturer, it is usually inspected, and everything it needs to function is built on the inside of it.

A lot of times, when we receive a product, we do not read the manual; it is not until something goes wrong with the product that we read the manual.

Manual: a book of instructions or a handbook that describes how the product works and its functions. Also, it gives us the history of the creator of the product and the mind of the creator of the product.

Most manufacturers also include a product warranty, guaranteeing their products will work. The warranty guarantees that if the product does not work in a certain amount of time, you could return it, replace it, or even get your money back.

Warranty: a formal promise or assurance that certain conditions will be fulfilled with the product; the product will be repaired or replaced if needed. In other words, if it's defective or something is wrong with it after it leaves the manufacturer.

The warranty also guarantees the assurance of the creator of the product; because his name is on the product, his reputation is on the line.

God is our creator, which means we are a product of God, and heaven is our manufactory; he created us in his image and likeness, had us on his mind, and the manual describes his mind **(Holy Scriptures).**

In the manual, we will find our purpose as a human being, how we should function, why we were created, our assignment, what we should be doing, how to do it, how to accomplish it, how to get it done, but ultimately and most of all our purpose of existence it's all in the manual.

When we purchase a product like a phone, car, or any device, it comes with a manual and a warranty. But a lot of people do not read the manual or warranty; the only thing some people are concerned with is how it works. Some will not read the manual even if something is wrong with it; most people go to someone else to fix the problem or ask someone for a solution.

The product's creator never intended for its user to go to others to ask how his product should function or its purpose. He built the product with everything it needed on the inside of it.

That is why it came with a manual and a warranty; the warranty guarantees that the product will work if we follow the instructions mentioned on the inside step by step.

You will never find a product asking another product how it should work (it just functions). Still, we find ourselves as human beings going to other products that our creator has created rather than the creator himself, the manual.

Just as a product may malfunction if not used according to its manual, so too can individuals experience negative consequences when they deviate from the prescribed path. This analogy suggests that seeking knowledge and guidance from reliable sources is crucial to avoid misinformation and potential pitfalls. It emphasizes the need for individuals to approach life with a sense of caution and discernment, ensuring that they align themselves with trustworthy sources of information and guidance.

God intends for all of us to follow the manual, His mind, purpose, will, and direction for our lives; studying the manual, the mind of our creator will reveal all that. The manual guarantees our success, and the warranty guarantees us abundant and everlasting life.

John 3:16 For God so loved the world, that he gave his only begotten son, that whosoever believeth in him should not perish, but have everlasting life.

Warranty: a formal promise or assurance that the product will fulfill certain conditions. If something is wrong with the product, the product will be repaired or replaced.

Also, it is a formal pledge to pay another person's debt or to perform another person's obligation in the case of default, defect, or malfunctioning.

"Jesus did it all for us."

Default: failure to fulfill an obligation, especially to repay a debt or appear in a court of law.

Defect: a shortcoming, imperfection, or lack of something necessary for completeness, flaw, imperfection, or weakness.

Malfunction: a failure to function in a normal or satisfactory manner, failure to function properly.

It also means defaulted or defective, which leads to malfunctioning. The cause and effects can be the wrong source of information, not following the manual and the original instructions of the creator.

But God, the creator of all things, loves his creation so much that he was willing to pay the debt for all our default defects, which lead us to malfunction. Which is the warranty that he guarantees the success of his product will function properly **(Jesus).**

That is why he loves the backslider and the sinner because the **(backslider & sinner)** are just products of the manufacturer that have been defective, defaulted, and malfunctioned.

Hosea 4:6 My people are destroyed for lack of knowledge because you have rejected knowledge, I will reject you from being my priest.

They do not understand the manual; that's why God called Preachers to share the **"Good News."** The **Kingdom of God** reveals the original instructions and restores original information.

1. Who are we **(God's Children)**
2. Where we came from **(God our Father in Heaven)**
3. What our purpose is **(to Glorify our Father God)**
4. How we should be functioning **(Follow the Manual)**
5. What our true abilities **are (be Productive, Multiply, Replenish, and Subdue the Earth)**
6. The power we have **(Dominion over the things on earth, not each other)**

We are King Kids...

Psalm 24:1 The Earth is the Lord's and the fullness of it, the world and they who dwell in it.

Roman 5:8 But God shows and clearly proves His **(own)** love for us by the fact that while we were still sinners, Christ **(the Messiah, the Anointed One)** died for us.

Jesus is the warranty; he paid the debt for all the default defects that caused the malfunction. If you just believe the warranty, trust it, and follow the original instructions, it guarantees our success in life; it is all a part of the manufacturer's plan in the manual.

John 15:7 If you abide in me and my words abide in you, you shall ask what you will, and it shall be done unto you.

The Word of God abides in the manual; Jesus was the manual, and he came to fulfill the manual, the Word of God/the original instructions.

John 1:1 In the beginning was the Word, and the Word was with God, and the Word was God.

14: and the word was made flesh and dwelt among us.

Jesus is the manual and the warrantee that guarantees our success.

When you build a product or building or a house, when there are defects or contamination in the construction of the building process, you need to repair the foundation and find the defects and repair them.

Some devices, products, buildings, or houses are refurbished, and some refurbished items can be just as good as the original. When something is refurbished, it is returned to the original manufacturer for repair to receive the original parts.

Refurbished: Renovate, recondition, revamp, restore, renew, redevelop, rebuild, reconstruct, and rehab to make something clean, bright, or fresh again.

The **Kingdom of God's Message** comes to refurbish us if we repent **(change our thinking)** and ask for forgiveness. God the Creator is faithful and just to forgive us, and He guarantees to cleanse us of all unrighteousness.

The Holy Spirit comes to remind us of the manual, cleanse us of all that inaccurate information, and make us more like the image he created us to be like God's children.

We were created in his image and likeness; the Holy Spirit comes to make us over, refurbish us, renovate us, abide in us, recondition, restore, renew, redevelop, rebuild, reconstruct us, and make us better for the **Kingdom of God**.